What Flower, Bush or Tree are YOU?

A Poetry Collection

MARIO PANAYI

Dedication

Dedicated to all the people whose name comes from a flower, bush or tree, especially my god-daughter's daughter, Amaryllis.

Contents

Aconitum (AKA Monkswood) 1

Alder Buckthorn Tree 3

Alder Tree 4

Amaryllis 5

American Beautyberry 6

Angel's Trumpet 7

Are you a Flower, Bush or Tree? 8

Aster 9

Autumn Crocus (AKA Fall Crocus, Naked Lady) 10

Azalea 11

Bamboo 12

Banana Shrub (Magnolia Figo) 13

Bay Laurel Tree 14

Beech Tree 16

Bird's Nest Fern 17

Bluebeard (Longwood Blue) 18

Bluebell 19

Bonsai 20

Bouquet 21

Bridal Wreath Shrub 22

Cactus 23

Cannabis 24

Carnation...25

Cedar Tree 26

Chinese Fringe Flower.....................................27

Chrysanthemum 28

Clover 29

Conifer 30

Conkers 31

Cotton Plant 33

Cypress 34

Daffodil...35

Dahlia..36

Daisy 37

Dandelion..38

Daphne 39

Devil's-Bit 40

Dogwood...41

Dwarf Lady Palm..42

Dwarf Smoke Bush 43

Elm Tree 44

Eucalyptus...45

Fairy Duster 46

Fern 47

Fig Leaf...48

Firecracker Flower 49

Fir Tree 50

(AKA Christmas Tree) 50

Flamingo Flower..51

Foxglove 52

Fuchsia...54

Garlic 55

Gladiolus..56

Granny's Bonnet...57

Grape Hyacinth...58

Heath..59

Heather...60

Hemlock...61

Henna 62

Hibiscus 63

Holly 64

Honesty (AKA Lunaria Annua/Annual Honesty) 65

Honeysuckle 66

Hyacinth...67

Hydrangea...68

Indian Hemp 69

Iris..70

Ivy..71

Japanese Andromeda 72

Jasmine 73

Latana 74

Lavender 75

Lilac 76

Lily...77

Lily of the Valley 78

Magnolia 79

Maple Tree..80

Marigold 81

Mistletoe 82

Monkey Puzzle Tree 83

Morel (AKA Morchella)..............................84

Morning Glory 85

Mother-of-the-Evening 86

Mountain Ash (AKA Rowan).......................87

Mountain Laurel 88

Myrtle 89

Nettle...90

Nicotiana (Tobacco Plant) 91

Nightshade 92

Oak Tree 93

Oleander...94

Orchid 95

Palm Tree...96

Pansy 97

Parsley..98

Passion Flower 99

Pine Tree 100

Poison Ivy 101

Pompom Weed...102

Poplar Tree...103

Poppy (from *Birth, Life Burial*) 104

Rhododendron..106

Rose 107

Rosemary 108

Scarlet Buckeye 109

Shamrock 110

Silver Birch 111

Skunk Weed..112

Smoke Tree...113

Snapdragon 114

Snowball Tree...115

Snowdrop..116

Spindle Tree 117

Spruce Tree...118

Strawberry Tree 119

Sugarcane...120

Sunflower..121

Sweet Pea 122

Sycamore 123

Thicket 124

Thistle 125

Thyme 126

Touch-Me-Not 127

Tulips 128

Violet 129

Viper's Grass 130

Virgin's Bower (AKA Devil's Hair, Love Vine) 131

Voodoo Lily (AKA Devil's Tongue, Snake Palm) 132

Water Lily 133

Water Lily (variant version) 134

Wildflowers 135

Willow 137

Wisteria 138

Witch Hazel 139

Yellow Bells 140

Yew 141

Yggdrasil 142

More Books by Mario...................................143

About the Author 152

Aconitum
(AKA Monkswood)

Just how old are you?
So many tales about you
Going back not years
Or even centuries
But eons ago

That Hecate
The granddaughter of Titans
Invented and created you
An alternative myth suggests
That you were created from
The burning saliva of Cerberus
The evil three-headed hound
Who viciously guarded Hades

Athena apparently used your poisons
To transform Arachne into a spider
Medea also using your poisons
Offering the hero Theseus
A cup of wine laced with aconite
Also known as Wolfsbane

You are later seen
In China and Japan
Still peddling your poisons
But also creating remedies
Then to modern times
Your poisons now so intense

That you administer
Not just through ingestion
But also through touching
The innocence of skin now
Becoming a lethal weapon of murder

So many details
Of your victim's deaths
Resulting in you reinventing yourself
Flowering and showering you
With nicknames galore;
Aconite, Monkshood, Wolfsbane,
Leopard's Bane, Mousebane
Woman's Bane, Devil's Helmet
Blue Rocket and of course
Queen of Poisons

But through it all
You have remained
Beautiful, mysterious
And always murderous

Alder Buckthorn Tree

Everything about you
Is smooth and suave
Nothing thorny about you
It's just not in your nature
Making you a bit of a rarity

Alder Tree

You seem to love the water
Whether it be streams
Or even dirty rivers
That's where you thrive
Making you a lover of life
Determined to grow and grow
By diving and making a splash
Rippling out your enthusiasm
Your energy being bountiful
Mesmerising and contagious

Amaryllis

Your name means pride and sparkle
You have much to be proud of
As you are stunning to look at
Yet your story began many eons ago
As a nymph in love with Alteo
Only the shepherd Alteo did not
Reciprocate that love
Amaryllis visited the house of Alteo
Each night piercing her heart
A drop of her blood would fall at his door
This continued for thirty nights
Until her yearning blood of desire
Sprouted into an amazing and dazzling flower

American Beautyberry

You are beautiful
The ultimate trophy wife
Or trophy girlfriend
Elegant, classy and sassy
Smooth skin and fresh fragranced
The sweetheart that everyone wants
Yet consuming too much of you
Is a recipe for becoming poisoned
Gut-wrenching aches of being seduced
By a toxic lover who is an expert
On ruining the lives of her conquests

Angel's Trumpet

You are clearly an offspring
From both Heaven and Hell
A beautiful looking Angel
With a natural fragrance
And soothing promises
Of eternal paradise

Oh those poor victims
Seduced by your appearance
Soon becoming delirious
Paralysed with hallucinations
Deranged and deluded visions
Unaware of their pending deaths

You can almost hear the chimes
Of death bells in the air
As you sway and hover
Above dying mortals
Always oozing beauty
Of an immortal Fallen Angel

Are you a Flower, Bush or Tree?

Flowers, bushes and trees
Are everywhere, contributing
To life on earth with pollination
With natural habitats
And with their beauty

Are you as fragrant as a flower?
Naturally sweet-scented
Beautiful to look at
A gift for amore
But occasionally
With a thorny side
To your character
Or even deceptively
Toxic and murderous

Perhaps you are like a bush
Thick, wiry and bushy unkempt hair
With an occasional trim
To look more alluring

Are you like a tree?
Tall and overshadowing
Spreading your branches
Leafy and relaxed
Swaying this way and that
With an occasional bark to your persona

Are you popular or a parasite?
Just how ambitious and successful are you?
Do you attract the birds and the bees?

Aster

You are special
Everything about you shines
Your destiny is obvious
You are a bright and shining star

Autumn Crocus
(AKA Fall Crocus, Naked Lady)

You are well into
Your *autumn* years
Showcasing your age
By dressing in pale lavender
Then shocking us all
With your *fall* from grace attitude
Getting *naked* and standing proud
Demonstrating that getting older
Doesn't mean *withering* away

Azalea

Beautiful
Intoxicating
Deadly
A deliverer
Of death threats
An executioner

Who could have imagined
That someone so beautiful
So mesmerising and alluring
Would have such a *shady* life
Making you nothing more
Than the ultimate bitch

Bamboo

You are tall and tough
Sturdy and attractive
Yet there is also a
Crunch to your character
And more worrying
Is that there is something
Hollow about you

But you are also
Exceptionally ambitious
Growing and spreading
At a rapid rate
Resulting in others wanting
To control and even curb
Your aggressive expansion

Your ability to adapt
To become creative
In so many *fields*
Including construction
Textiles and even food
Means that you are resilient
A genuine survivor through the ages

Banana Shrub
(Magnolia Figo)

You are beautiful
With soft leathery skin
Natural intoxicating aroma

Despite being tough
You are easy to take care of
Making you classy and elegant

You might have a natural gloss
But at times you blush, my petal
Showcasing your vulnerability

Bay Laurel Tree

There is a Myth of Ancient Greece
An ill-fated love story
Of Apollo and Daphne
It begins with an argument
Between the Gods Apollo and Eros
Insults are hurled
Over their combined love for archery
Vengeance is obtained by Eros
For he shoots one of his love arrows
At Apollo making him fall in love with Daphne
But another arrow made of lead
Is shot at the river nymph
Instilling heavy hatred in her heart towards Apollo

Apollo pursues Daphne
But she is dedicated to sports and the forests
Into her beloved forests she runs to escape
Pursued by the amorous-ichor fuelled Apollo
Eros determined to cause more conflict
Causes Daphne to stumble
Distraught as Apollo is catching up to her
She prays and begs Mother Earth
To save her from Apollo
Even if it means swallowing her into the earth
Or transforming into something else
Her prayers are answered
Cruelly becoming a Laurel Bay Tree

Daphne's transformation is agonising
Feet merging into the soil

Splintering into roots
Legs and body becoming hard
As smooth skin turns into rough bark
Arms becoming branches
Fingers transforming into spiny twigs
Hair turning into green leaves
Whilst those sparkling eyes that shined
Close and when they reopen
They bloom into magnificent flowers
And so the magic of myth
Creates the evergreen Bay Laurel Tree

The story does not end there
For Apollo, god of music, archery, poetry
Prophecy, the sun and athletics
Is still enamoured by the tree
He vows to Daphne that he will always love her
Always honour her by wearing the Bay Laurel leaves
Like a crown in his hair and sing songs about Daphne
Apollo uses his divinity to bestow immortality
Upon the Bay Laurel Tree and makes her evergreen
Despite the eons that have passed
You can still smell her natural sweet fragrance
You can still sense her deep fear and panic
As she sways trembling in the wind

Beech Tree

Despite your age
You are strong
A grafter on many levels
Contributing to the economy
And may I say
You are also smoking hot

Bird's Nest Fern

You have crinkled skin
Perhaps an indication
Of the years you have spent
Providing nests to so many

You are genuinely kind
Possessing a natural ability
To look after and nurture
Even those you are not related to

Bluebeard (Longwood Blue)

Just looking at you
Or being in your company
Makes me feel relaxed

Your natural beauty
Misty strong fragrance
Makes you heavenly

Bluebell

You are shy
Always looking down
As though ashamed of yourself
Yet you are beautiful

If you continue to droop
You'll end up like that permanently
You have a sweet-innocent scent
Is that what led to your downfall?

You could easily be the belle of the ball
But you continue to hide away
It's almost as though you are ashamed
Dear Beautiful Bluebell, what happened?

I shudder in delight when in your company
I shudder in fright thinking what happened
To make you so sheltered and virtually endangered
Look up and you just might find your *Happy Ever After*

Bonsai

You are petite
But so beautiful
That you are
Living Art

You are
Aesthetically perfect
That it looks as though
You have been pruned

You are stylish
Clearly maintained
Classy and elegant
Whilst remaining rooted

Darling, you belong
In a museum
So that all can view
And appreciate your beauty

Bouquet

You give your woman a bouquet
Along with chocolates such as Milk Tray
Which will absolutely make her day
Unless of course it's an apology you're trying to sway

You can give other presents such a perfume to spray
Or lingerie that's sexy, alluring and risqué
Arrange a meal at a restaurant that's gourmet
But NOT toothpaste to fight tooth decay

Put your emotions on display
That you love her and will never betray
Stay faithful until your dying day you'll convey
Hoping to please her and not cause rolling eyes of dismay

Pop the question and internally pray
That *yes* is what she will reply and say
Remember having a calm day is a cliché
As it will always begin with giving her a bouquet

Bridal Wreath Shrub

You are conflicted
Showcasing the happiness
Of a bride on her wedding day
Blossoming in a white dress
And a white drooping veil
Then exhibiting a mournful look
Shadowed in the dark torments
Of death and mourning
As though carrying
A wreath at a funeral
Feet sinking and rooted
Into the soil of a grave

You are beautiful
Shining bright
But your thoughts
Those internal demons
Will haunt you
And so you continue
To waver between
Happiness and sadness
Shimmering in and out of the light
A bi-polar existence
A bride weighed down
By a wretched wreath

Cactus

You are sharp
So cutting
Prickly
No one could accuse you
Of being spineless
Dry and hollow
Able to survive
In even desolate conditions
Which is so apt
Because being so vitriolic
You will always lead
A lonely and solitary life

Cannabis

You are not exactly
The best looker
And yet there is something
Very addictive about you
You relax me
Take me to a happy place
I feel like I could eat you
Inhale your very essence
There is a smouldering
Smoky atmosphere
Whenever I am in your company
You're bad for me
So very, very bad
I forget all my commitments
Yet I keep coming back for more
You are my guilty pleasure
My illegal lover

Carnation

There is something sexy about you
You're soft and cuddly
Smooth to touch
Colourful and vibrant
And you smell amazing

But there is also something very sad
For if I trace your ancestry
There are stories that your lineage
First arrived when a mother
Watched her only son being crucified

Yet there are other stories
About the origins of your genealogy
That the goddess Diana was rejected
By a shepherd boy on whom she took revenge
Ripping out his eyes and his splattered
Blood gave rise to your kind

All these stories do not deter me from you
For you are still beautiful and radiant
Freshening up my day

Cedar Tree

Tall and broad
With a spicy scent
And a natural ability
For athletics

Often found in the mountains
Where you are at ease
As though that is
Where you belong

Your characteristics
Have survived for centuries
Not only making you a survivor
But adaptable and capable

No doubt you are excellent
At woodwork and creating furniture
Making you an ideal prospect
To work as a carpenter of course

Chinese Fringe Flower

You are deeply colourful
With your abrasive
And acidic character
Yet you are still
So very appealing
Beautiful and sexy
Enticing paramours
All because you are
Naturally naughty

Chrysanthemum

You are a healer
Soothing away pains
Relieving aches
Making me feel youthful
Spritely and energetic
Your beauty and radiance
Has revitalised me
You brighten my day
Giving me a reason
To live life to the full

Clover

You live a leafy and relaxed life
Always at ease and with good humour
Almost impossible to offend

You are carefree and satisfied with life
Behaving as though you are the luckiest in the world
What a wonderful and rare thing your outlook is

Conifer

You are really, really tall
Hiding your real *bark*
With an ability to *needle* others
Causing them to *pine* over you

Conkers

You drive me conkers
Standing tall as though out of reach
Making me jump up and down
Even throw a stick at you
Gently hitting your limbs
Make a whistling sound in the air
Just to get your prickly attention

Do I need to make you fall to the ground?
Hurt my fingers whilst trying
To unravel your prickly exterior
It's as though you have become acidic
Dipped and boiled in vinegar
Creating your hardened attitude

Do I need to drill a hole?
Into that thick brick head of yours
To find your softer interior
Put a string through the hole
And swing and flick you around
Hitting you again and again
Until I break that hard shell exterior

Did you have no childhood?
Do I need to give you a childhood?
Create fun games of precision
Where you can hear the laughter of children
As they play their childhood games
Living their lives of innocence
Before adulthood and responsibility arrives

Have I hit the nail on the head?
Were you actually hit as a child?
Over and over again with a hard stick
Oh, what caused you to be so?
You do continue to drive me conkers

Cotton Plant

You are so soft
That you have become fluffy
To the very *fibre* of your being

Your ability to spin a *yarn*
Has made you popular
Throughout the entire world

People spend their money
To have you in their life
Right next to their body

Cypress

You are forever green
The colour of envy
So jealous of others
That you are determined
To grow and grow
Becoming the tallest
And the strongest
In all the land

Daffodil

You are dazzling
Bright as the sun
You are Narcissus
Looking into the river
Mesmerised by your own reflection
Youthful and handsome
But if you share his arrogance
Then you are doomed
For he wasted away
Falling in love with himself
Growing weaker and weaker
A sad and lonely death
Next to a river with
The gold-yellow flowers

Dahlia

You are a survivor
Prone to illness and disease
But each time you come back stronger
Rejuvenated and reinventing yourself
You are the perfect friend and lover
Beautiful in every way
Including your empathy and compassion
Perhaps because of what you have endured

Daisy

You are colourful and innocent
Pure as a child when playing
I could almost visualise
A chain of daisies
Running through the fields
Or a young boy in a straw hat and shorts
Plucking the petals of a white flower
As he daydreams about you
Saying the words over and over
She loves me, she loves me not
She loves me, she loves not
Until he plucks the last petal
Determining your destiny

Dandelion

You behave as though
Born and raised in the wild
Wandering through rain and wind
Living the life of a Romany Gypsy
Granting wishes and dreams
Curing illnesses with your herbal remedies
Even selling your own homemade brews

Daphne

You are beautiful
But something traumatic
Has happened in your life
To make you an expert
In discreetly delivering
Poisons and toxins
Into the bloodstream
Of anyone who comes near you
Resulting in them suffering
Debilitating diseases and pain
And sometimes even death
Causing burning sensations
Unsightly and agonising lesions
Irreversible damage to organs
Including kidneys and the heart
A coma that you cannot recover from
Such severe witch-like concoctions
Enough to drive an Olympian god mad
Dear Daphne, were your laurel leaves
Responsible for the disappearance
Of Apollo and all of his fellow Olympians?

Devil's-Bit

You had a natural ability
To cure those who were suffering
Carefully soothing their pain
Healing them to health

You cared and cured so many
That you caught the attention
Of the devil who raged
Furious flames flared within him

Upon arriving on earth
The Father and King of Hell
Attempted to caress and cajole you
Temptation and torture techniques failed

In anger he resorted to biting
But even that was not enough
As you continued in your endeavours
Whilst the devil turned a permanent shade of red

Dogwood

You are a mystery
A mixture of being
Dense, hard and strong
Thick, fruity and medicinal
Yet there is also something
Fine about you, which is why
You are also popular
Or am I getting popular
Mixed up with being common?

Dwarf Lady Palm

You have an expensive nature
Enjoying a glossy foundation
You are delicate and deep
A woman through and through
Having men in the very *palm*
Of your hand, and eventually
They become *dwarfed*
Attending to your requirements
Merely existing in your shadow

Dwarf Smoke Bush

You have the heightened
And dangerous spirit
Of smoke and fires
Yet there is no real toxicity

Vibrant flames rising within
Hot, burning and scalding
But those who take the time
Soon realise the truth of you

For the smoke and fires transform
Into something amazing and beautiful
Passion furiously raging
Amorous, tender and fulfilling

Elm Tree

You have grown tall
Really, really tall
But sadly you have
Become susceptible
To disease and potential death
Luckily for you
You are currently in remission
Appearing strong and sturdy
Oblivious to others
What you have gone through
The worry and the pain
Stay strong and sturdy
Take care of yourself
Despite your nature
To stay rooted to one spot
Live life to the full

Eucalyptus

You are a survivor
And very much
A lover of new techniques

You are adaptable
Having learned to survive
Through the most awful fires

You deny having plastic surgery
And yet it's as though you shed your skin
Every year new and younger-looking skin

You love essential oils
It's almost as though
You create those oils yourself

Fairy Duster

You love living in the heat
That's when you absolutely thrive
Your favourite colour is pink

The birds, the bees and the deer
All love to get a taste of you
Which you never object to

Fern

You are distinctive
Instantly recognisable
Stylish and resilient
For you do not put up
With annoying pests
They'll soon give up
Unable to destroy you
Move onto someone else
Someone they can infest

Your origins are a mystery
Myths galore have spread
Suggesting you are magical
Able to exorcise evil
Drive away slithering snakes
And other slimy creatures
Which is why you continue
To survive and prosper
Despite being rooted

So perhaps the secret
To your longevity
Is being unadventurous

Fig Leaf

No matter how large the fig leaf you find
With your personality and antics
You will never, ever
Find a fig leaf large enough
To hide away all that shame

Firecracker Flower

You are erect
Against my dishevelled petals
As though windswept

When I'm no longer in my prime
Dried up and discarded
That's when I explode

You may call me your flower
Or your firecracker
But you made me what I am

Fir Tree
(AKA Christmas Tree)

You stand so tall
Green with envy
As children play
At the level of your feet
You give people the brush off
Standing stoically and standoffishly still
Pretending you do not notice anyone

What do I need to do to get you to notice me?
Sit on the ground and unwrap presents
Gather my family and eat in your presence
Laugh and play games underneath you
Run around wrapping you up in tinsel
Maybe even flashing lights

Start relaxing and join in the festivities
You might even find yourself
Your very own beautiful fairy

Flamingo Flower

You look so hot
Flaming and smouldering
Igniting men's hearts
As they melt like wax
To your demands

You love and live life to the full
Exhibiting your beauty
Indoors and outdoors
Exuberant and extrovert
Avant-garde

Yet there is also something
Dangerous about you
Discarding your conquests at a whim
Leaving them destroyed as though poisoned
Whilst you move on to man after man

Foxglove

You are beautiful
Once thought
To be innocent
Even medicinal
Oh, how wrong
That perception was

Beautiful, yes
But deadly
A femme fatale
Making men's hearts
Race or even stop
With no remorse

You are as cunning
As a fox wearing gloves
To silence the pitter patter
Sounds of their feet
As they approach
Their victims

They say that you administer
Poison through the skin
Earning you the nickname
Of Witch's Glove
Having avoided
Poisoning yourself

There is also a myth
That as your victims die

You are in the fields
Your dress swaying
Almost like a silent bell
A Dead Man's Bells

Fuchsia

You are bright and bold
A fusion of royal purple
And devil red

Garlic

You make me feel
So healthy and alive
And I certainly
Enjoy the taste of you
Cheeky and spicy
But all of this activity
It makes you smell
Well …….
Overwhelmingly
…….. pungent
Sorry. Sorry. Sorry.

Gladiolus

Can I call you Gladys?
Or Glad for short?
And you do make me feel glad
With your bright and vibrant
Colourful personality
But you can also be
As sharp as a sword
Cutting me down
Luckily that sword
Is usually in its sheath
But just knowing
Of the existence of the blade
Keeps me in check
And that's just how you like it

Granny's Bonnet

You take me back in time
To a bygone era
A time of innocence
When people were friendly
Towards one another
Willing to be helpful

You make me feel as though
I am in the countryside
Breathing in fresh air
Fields with long blades of uncut grass
And flowers in bloom adding to the scent

I can almost hear birds whistling
In rustling trees and visualise a stream
Children playing in the fields
Chasing each other or picking wildflowers
Young lovers hidden away
Kissing, cuddling and caressing
Whilst families elsewhere have picnics
Paper plates with sandwiches and cakes
An old man sleeps and snores
Whilst an elderly woman tries to hold on
To her flowery-coloured bonnet and dress
As the wind cheekily whisks around her

Grape Hyacinth

At times you might look
As though feeling blue
Drooped and depressed
But the sun brings out
The very best in you
Spring to early winter
You are in full bloom
I could get drunk on you
Bite and gobble you up
But would you leave
A sour taste in me?
Making me feel as though
Turned upside down

Heath

You are common
Uncultivated and overgrown

You are rough and tough
Coarse and dry

But through it all
You are authentic and natural

Heather

You have no airs and graces
Quite happy to be in heathlands
Or moorlands and even in a bog
Relaxing in open nature
Grazing lazily in fields
Yet you have the ability
To easily reinvent yourself
From looking rugged and dishevelled
To brushing away that image
With a burning new one
A beauty amongst the ordinary

Hemlock

Despite your innocent look
Which you have perfected
You cannot help yourself
Having become exceptionally
Dangerous and toxic

Every fibre within you
Is full of murderous intent
It is in your nature
You are nothing more
Than a vicious killer

Henna

You are determined
To place your mark on me
Becoming a decorated part of you

Your hold over me will be temporary
Because ultimately
I value my independence

But then again, I also value you
Resulting in our relationship
Resuming from time to time

I stay away from you
For most of the year
Because our union is to *dye* for

Hibiscus

You love warm and tropical climates
Wearing loud and brash colours
To suit your personality
You are a natural beauty
And you know it
But still you plaster yourself
With thick make-up
To accentuate your image
As dangerous and as an enigma

Holly

You are beautiful to look at
But you are also
Dangerous and thorny
Willing to draw blood
Without any remorse

You behave all majestic
Regal as though a crown
Fit for an omnipotent king
However, you are deceptive
Merely a crown of thorns

Honesty
(AKA Lunaria Annua/Annual
Honesty)

You are mysterious
So many stories about you
Folk tales and theories

You are a good luck charm
Bringing luck and money
To those who are seduced by you

There are rumours
That you are a witch
Able to keep monsters away

There is even speculation
That you are a descendant
Of Judas Iscariot

That story suggests you still possess
The thirty pieces of silver
Which explains your alleged powers

Whilst others say
You are completely mad
From years of staring at the moon

Let's face it
You spread all those rumours
Be *honest*, who are you?

Honeysuckle

You have a natural fragrance
Drawing me near to you
Like the sailors to the sirens

There is something delicious about you
Almost as though you are
The nectar of the gods

Just thinking about you
Makes me climb up the walls
I could hum about you all day long

Hyacinth

There is a story
From ancient myth
About a prince called Hyacinth
Who dared to love a god
When Hyacinth died
In the arms of his lover
The god turned his blood
Into the hyacinth flower
And the petals of those flowers
Are purposely curled
To remind Apollo
Of his lover's hair

Hydrangea

You are the ultimate example
That no one can survive without water
It is part of our DNA

Everyone knows
That without water we will wilt
Death and decomposing into the soil

Yet your thirst for water is to the extreme
It is as though you are having
The ultimate passionate love affair

Indian Hemp

You have an unusual effect on me
Becoming like a sedative
Almost as though
Listening to rustling leaves
You've become hypnotic
My heart rhythm slows down
As my mind wanders off

Perhaps it's time to rethink
To re-evaluate
Make new decisions
Whether to continue our union
As the song plays in my head
Whilst you continue to rustle
Should I stay, or should I go?

Iris

You are like a rainbow
Or a caring goddess
Adding brightness
In the most
Depressing circumstances

You would cross a dry desert
A rocky mountain, meadowlands
Bogs and even riverbanks
To add colour
To a dry, barren life

Your eye misses nothing
Giving out thoughtful gifts
From perfumes and aromatherapy
Essential oils and alcoholic gins
To medicines for those who are ill

Ivy

You are adorable to look at
Initially a friend who is comforting
And that's how you progress
Slyly shooting across into lives
Using a variety of techniques
Becoming rampant and clinging
Unhinged and unruly
As you begin to suffocate others
Even willing to strangulate
Mightily climbing ladders
Not caring if you bring down rivals
Or even friends and relatives
And so you need to come with a warning

Japanese Andromeda

So beautiful
Yet so deadly

The ultimate example
Of a *Femme Fatale*

Jasmine

You are perfume scented
A natural aroma that flows
Your fragrance being
So real and addictive

You are innocent and white
But occasionally you can be
Vibrant and bright as yellow
In your cheeky antics

Then there are those times
When you go beyond cheeky
Naughty and mischievous
Leading to you blushing red

Latana

You are certainly colourful
Very difficult to miss or ignore
To the extent that you can become
Irritating and annoying like a rash

Lavender

You have a unique sweet
And intoxicating fragrance
Aromatic to the extreme

You are so perfect
That everyone wants you
Squeezing you so hard
That drop by drop
They have squeezed
The very essence out of you

They want you to spread
All over their bodies
Almost like transforming you
Into smooth and sexy perfumed oils

Lilac

Purple in ancient times
Was the colour for royalty
And you do ooze nobility
And as for your scent
Intoxicating
Fresh and crisp
Drawing men to you
But only those that are handsome
And rich stand a chance
For you have a regal status
That you want to obtain
But all of the above
Comes with a severe warning
For in ancient times
Royalty was not just associated with wealth
But with danger and even murder

Lily

You are the only one
Capable of making
Freckles look
Incredibly sexy

Lily of the Valley

There is something
Very tender about you
Delicate and vulnerable

You can almost hear
The sound of bells softly
Whistling in the winds

You are both majestic looking
And locked in mourning
As though fearful of living

Magnolia

You are far older
Than your appearance
You are amazing
In whatever colour
You choose to wear

You are medicinal
With your ability to soothe
You are brash and proud
Bi-sexuality is not an issue
As you stand tall and sturdy

You are able to amalgamate
Being tough with grace
You are without doubt
The ultimate survivor
And you are beautiful

Maple Tree

You are striking
So striking that you could
Become a national symbol

You are desirable
Your ability to create
Something so sumptuous
Is worth millions and millions

But as with all genuine celebrities
You have merely become a commodity
Carved into what others want you to be

Marigold

You are beautiful
Valued like precious gold
Which results in suitors
Including pests
So you have developed techniques
To deal with those parasitic worms
Wearing a perfume that is pungent
Or just your natural musky scent
That makes you so, so brave

Mistletoe

You are beautiful to look at
Temptation and alluring
Yet the truth is you can be toxic
Lovers you amass
Sweet kisses you deliver
As you draw them in
So innocent looking
So much to offer
Your love affairs
Are going one way only
Because you are the ultimate
Example of a parasitic lover
Draining the very essence
Of all those you have seduced
Showing no regret or remorse
Growing in strength and popularity
Whilst the numbers of your victims
Continue to grow and spread

Monkey Puzzle Tree

You are thick and tough
Reptilian and jagged
Sharp and very noticeable

They don't make them like you anymore
Perhaps that's why you are sometimes
Referred to as a *Living Fossil*

Morel
(AKA Morchella)

Many consider you a fungi
Unwashed and dirty
But if they took the time
To have fun washing you
Becoming intimate
Discovering the scrumptious you
You are truly gourmet
Bella, Bella, Beautiful Morchella

Morning Glory

You are bright and alert
From the earliest hours
In the morning
Feeling invigorated and fresh
As though dripping
With the dew from your garden
You are a colourful character
In full bloom throughout the day
Enjoying life to the full
Permanently in high spirits
Loving life and giving others
A bright start to their day

Mother-of-the-Evening

You give yourself
In plentiful amounts
Generating amazing fragrances

You are vibrant and colourful
Becoming most vivacious and active
During the evenings

Your reputation has made you
Both popular and unpopular
With some wanting to eradicate you

But you continue being you
Conquering new lovers
And *leafing* them with a bitter taste

Mountain Ash
(AKA Rowan)

You are so strong
That you are capable
Of crucifying
The most powerful

It would not be a surprise
To those who know you
To discover that you could even
Make a god bleed, drip by drip

You have got the ability
To be a cruel murderer
Nailing and hammering your victims
So that they cannot escape

Giving them a slow and agonising death
Deluded in your belief
That you are an executioner
Of those who deserve to die

Mountain Laurel

You have a love of mountains
Finding you on rocky slopes
And in mountain forests
A haven for hikers

Is that where you learnt your skills?
Toxins capable of killing
Small and large animals
Including humans

You are beautiful
Innocent looking
With those young freckles
Yet a deceptive silent killer

Perhaps that is how
You manage to kill and kill again
Your victims staggering off
Suffering a lonely and agonising death

Whilst you continue to prosper
Healthy and blooming
No evidence of the darkness within you
Making you a secretive psychopathic killer

Myrtle

You are a rarity
Believing in fidelity
In love and marriage
In good luck and prosperity
Treating tradition and vows as sacred
No trace of jealousy or hatred
Like a flower rooted in soil
You are gentle and loyal
Capable of worshipping others
You are a genuine star

Nettle

You have a reputation
Of being stinging
Like several needles
Injected into the skin
All at the same time
Causing others pain
They become itchy
Scratching erratically
You remain unaffected
Stubbornly rooted
As though too proud
To even show affection

Nicotiana (Tobacco Plant)

You are bad for me
And yet you are also
My naughty addiction
As I bring you to my lips

Inhaling your scent
A burning yearning
Taking me to heaven
And then to hell

You make men feel manly
Women feel womanly
And young adults to feel
They could conquer the world

I sometimes want to give you up
And other times want you forever
But my biggest fear is
You just might be the death of me

Nightshade

You are an enigma
Occasionally having a reputation
For being deadly, sinister and toxic
Completely venomous and ruthless

Yet you are also considered
Beautiful, calm and unassuming
Wonderful to be around
Soothing and delightful

At other times
There are examples
That you are like tasty food
Allowing men and women to take a bite

So many stories
You have perfected
The art of no one discovering
Who the real you is

Oak Tree

It may take months
And even years and years
But you are an example
Of enduring patience and belief
No matter what your humble beginnings are
Persevere and persevere
Grow little by little
Protect yourself
And slowly
You will grow
Strong and sturdy
With a legacy to leave

Oleander

You are beautiful
Luring people in
Until they have a taste of you
Bitter to the extreme
And if they overcome that bitterness
Determined to taste you again and again
You will become more than just bitter
You will become venomous
Making you nothing more
Than the ultimate tease

Orchid

There is something exotic about you
Intriguing and entertaining
Exceptional beauty
Colourful and vibrant
Determined to live life to the full
With a natural intoxicating fragrance
There is a semblance and suggestion
Of hidden wildness within you
What I have yet to discover
Is whether you are kind or dangerous?

Palm Tree

Every time I see you
You bring sunshine to my life
By the beaches and the sea
Walking barefoot on the sand
Swimming in salty ocean clear blue waters
Enjoying a mojito or other cocktail
Feeling fresh and alive
And of course
Happiness unbound
Whilst in your company

Pansy

You are considered flimsy-looking
Colourful, vibrant and vivaciously shocking
In fields and gardens you love dancing and shimmering

You have been called so many names
It's hard to recall all those attempts at shame
Heart's-ease, Humble Violet, Step-Mother, and Little
Flame

You are so much more than just the colours you wear
Having overcome illnesses and pests, enough to make you
swear
You are truly beautiful, resilient and strong, and people do
actually care

Parsley

You are the ultimate victim
Bright and healthy-looking
Yet soon cut down whilst young
Cut and diced and crushed
Becoming a meal of desire
For others to satisfy their hunger
Until you disappear completely

Passion Flower

You are distinctive
Unusual looking
Hypnotic and mesmerising
Drawing people in

Once wild and exotic
Eventually tamed
But still exhibiting
Flame-fuelled passion

Pine Tree

You have lived a long life
Both joyous and full of strife
Seen the world evolve
But refused to get involved

Season after season
Decade after decade
Wars justified with reason
Real memories beginning to fade

Rough and tough skin
Worn and torn over the years;
Now flaky and scaly
Bristly and gristly

Do you reminisce?
The years full of bliss?
Spending all of your time
With memories as you pine

Poison Ivy

You are innocent looking
But you might as well
Be at a masquerade
Secretly and deliberately
Administering poison

You are an irritant
Like a rash or blister
After contact with you
I either want a cold shower
Or to grab a bottle of alcohol

You are beautiful
But even one touch
Of your smooth beauty
Leaves me with regret
Stinging sensations of shame

You are one who needs
To be avoided, but in reality
With deceptive charms
You grab your victim's attention
And then leave your mark

You ensure you will
Always be remembered
Alluring and enticing
The ultimate example
Of beauty is skin deep

Pompom Weed

You are a survivor
To the detriment of others
Destroying them completely
Basking gloriously in sun and rain
Content in your amazing abilities
Unaware of your loneliness
And of your immense depression
Resulting in you hibernating
Withdrawn and disappearing
Until you revive and rebound
A spectacular return
In your bright and vivacious colours
Once again determined to destroy
As everyone is seen as a potential rival
The life and times of a pompom princess

Poplar Tree

Tall
Dark
Smooth

That's why
You are
So popular

Poppy
(from *Birth, Life Burial*)

In ancient myth
Even before the Olympians lived
The poppy thrived
Used by Hypnos, the god of dreams
Its potent narcotic seeds
Sending gods and mortals to their sleep

In the midst of wars
Where streams of blood
Have replaced roads and homes
Where the dust has replaced clean air
There is only one thing that grows
The resilient poppy

To alleviate the agony
Of those dying and in pain
The unripe seedpods of the poppy are used
Developing medicinal morphine
Treating those who are suffering
Easing the chronic torment that they face

Profiteering from the illegal trafficking
Of heroin created by the opium of the poppy
Injected, smoked, inhaled and snorted
For the euphoric highs
Followed by the lows
Addiction, ruined lives and premature deaths

It was the scene from Flanders Fields
A sea of poppies blowing in the winds
With their flimsy blood-coloured petals
The only living thing not to have perished
Symbolising the eternal spirit of the soldiers
Wearing it with pride will always be the poppy

Rhododendron

Beautiful

But

Dangerous

Rose

You are elegant
Full of fragrance
Intoxicating
A heaven-sent gift
Sexy and alluring
Virtually an aphrodisiac

You look beautiful and glamorous
In whatever colour you wear
White, yellow, orange, pink
However, it is red that is your true fame
The colour of blood, the devil and danger
Which of course you are more than capable of

You have a delicate nature
Smooth and soft like velvet
Fragile as butterfly wings
But also vehemently protective
A thorny side to your character
Even capable of drawing blood

Rosemary

You are well known
Traditional and modern
For example you are at home
In kitchens where food is prepared
With old-fashioned herbs
Adding flavour and spice
And you are also adept
At adorning essential oils
Aromatic fragrance-fuelled perfumes

Yes, you are well known throughout the world
And will remain well known
Until the day you die
But your fame is of the calibre
That you are also immortal
As you will continue
To be present in so many lives
Enhancing the richness
Of their daily routines

Scarlet Buckeye

You have the colour
Of the devil and his demons
In your soul and spirit
Dark, dark red

You are attractive
Your bad reputation
Attracts both the birds
And the stinging bees

You have a wild nature
Quite often poisonous
Able to inflict
Cruel pain and agony

Despite the obvious pleasures
That you offer in abundance
When you leave it can be messy
Yet your popularity continues

Shamrock

You are very distinctive
Immediately associated
With being Irish

I can visualise you
On the Emerald Isle
In a sea of shimmering clovers

He or she who finds you
Will feel like the luckiest
Person in the entire world

Silver Birch

You are tall and slender
Almost anaemic looking
Yet you are stunning
Amazing and spectacular
Such a beauty

Skunk Weed

You stink
Like a skunk
Such a strong odour
That it's having
A psychedelic effect on me
And everyone near you

Smoke Tree

You are like a cloud
Retaining your angst
Then when it becomes
So overwhelming
Those tears run like floods

You are like a fire
Raging bright
But when you decide to vent
All that smoke
Is what can make you lethal

Snapdragon

You are really just a softy
Smooth and velvety
Pretending to roar
To be a dragon
Amusing children
And adults too
That makes you a people person
A carer and someone who values others
Not many have those qualities
Making you very special
With a beautiful soul and spirit

Snowball Tree

You appear innocent
But just like white snow
Where children love to play
Your appearance might be deceptive
Causing others to slip and slide
To fall and bruise
Just saying
I'm still undecided
Still not sure about the real you

Snowdrop

You are so innocent
That you are drooped
As though in sorrow
Or ashamed to exist

You are so beautiful
That anyone else
Would be excessively
Proud and boastful

Being so naïve
Makes it dangerous
The potential for you
To be pulled away
From your natural home

Gathered with others
Of a similar nature
Becoming fragile and cold
Desperately leaning
On each other for support

A new existence
With a limited lifespan
Slowly wilting away
Until …… no more
Disappearing
Like melted snow

Spindle Tree

You are bright
Exceptionally sharp
Deceptively alluring
Attractive and stunning

Winter resistant
Hard and resilient
Absorbing extreme weather
Including frost and winds

Icy words and deeds
Are no match for you
You have years of experience
Cutting and slicing egos

Spin it any way you want
Because you can be
Just as bitter as anyone else
And even become poisonous

Spruce Tree

Everything about you
Is how parental you are
Providing a home for all
Comfy and snug
Nourishing food
And when those
Little ones move on
Will you end up
Pining after them?

Strawberry Tree

You are self-sufficient
Able to live and thrive
In many types of conditions
But you love the sun most of all
A Mediterranean lifestyle
With sun, sea and strawberries

Sugarcane

You are naturally sweet
So sugary-sweet that
I become either
Hypoactive
Excitable
Intensely alert
Or I become
Overdosed on sucrose
Rotting away inside
As though heading
To become comatose

Sunflower

You stand tall and proud
Protruding your neck
As though superior
Just like a giraffe
Regal and rooted
However,
It wasn't that long ago
Back in your younger years
When your head would tilt
Chasing the sunshine
Or were you eyeing-up
Those who were too afraid
To approach you
Or perhaps even
Turning your back on them
Yet somehow
Despite your deluded status
You managed to procreate
Unfortunately,
They too followed your lead
Standing tall
With their faces
Chasing the sun

Sweet Pea

You are beautiful
Strong sense of colour
Matching that strong fragrance
You could seduce just about anyone
My sweet, sweet pea

Sycamore

You are large, strong and broad
Once smooth skinned
But with age that skin
Has begun to flake
But that is just a sign
That with age comes wisdom
Because you are still standing
Still just as strong in mind and spirit

Thicket

You are very dense
Standing tall and wide
Almost intimidating to look at
Which means people avoid you
Resulting in quite a lonely existence

You're a little bit scruffy looking
Unshaven long and wiry hair
Perhaps if you had a trim
You might make yourself
More appealing

Still exhibiting your brusque demeanour
But with a more metrosexual stance
A refined stubble look
Instead of a macho brute
Who could do with a bath
A shave and a splash of body spray

But the reality is
The closest you will get to that
Is to stand rooted to the spot
Whilst the rain washes over you

Thistle

You are sharp
And prickly
Inflicting pain
Your ability
To agonise others
Is legendary

Yet despite
Your natural
Characteristics
You still manage
To attract the birds
And the butterflies

Thyme

You are dry
Really, really dry
And that's what makes you
Completely medicinal

Touch-Me-Not

You are so shy
As soon as someone
Comes near to you
You become withdrawn
Almost as though
Folding yourself inside-out
Regressing to the foetal position
Safe within mummy's womb
Becoming sleepy and sensitive
Shimmering cold and afraid
Of being touched
Creating rumours
That you are so shy
You will never experience
The shame and joy
Of becoming intimate

Tulips

You are popular
Beautiful and amazing
Dazzling and seductive
With a fresh fragrance
Radiating sultry temptation
Resulting in you conquering
The entire world

Violet

Your scent is flirtatious
As it breezes around
Capturing admirers
You are wickedly adventurous
A lover of men and women
Discarding lover after lover

You have charisma
Able to express emotions
Desire and passion
Through music and lyrics
Virtually becoming divine
As though a tenth secret muse

Yet there is also a legend
That you will fall in love
Be rejected and haunted
By images of former lovers
Finally realising the importance
And worth of true love

Viper's Grass

You might be petite
But you have mastered
Hiding your true characteristics
Like a snake in grass
Poised and ready
To launch their attack
Stinging their victim
With a lethal bite
Before devouring them whole

Virgin's Bower
(AKA Devil's Hair, Love Vine)

You are aggressive
Twisting and twirling
Into the lives of others
Unashamedly encroaching
Virtually strangulating them

Beautiful, but also dangerous
Pretending to be shy
Coy and virginal
Before unleashing
The devil within

Voodoo Lily
(AKA Devil's Tongue, Snake Palm)

You are unusual and distinctive looking
Tall and vivacious with a sad history
Having been used and abused
You have lashed out without wanting to
You are a prime example
Of unintentional murder

Lives have changed forever
For you and your victim
Friends and family of both
Are haunted forever more
Living in the shadows
Of one dramatic event

Whilst those with a devil's tongue
Descendants of a slithering serpent
Who cajoled and persuaded a woman
To infamously fall from grace
Continue in their endeavours
To destroy more and more lives

Water Lily

You are a natural mermaid
Beautiful, svelte and mesmerising
Loving the water
Almost as though you and the water
Are having a love affair
Becoming as one
Unable to live without each other

Water Lily
(variant version)

You are beautiful
But for whatever reason
You are drowning
Struggling to cope with life
Trying to survive
With your head barely
Above the water

Wildflowers

You are a free spirit
With your natural perfumed scent
Drawing me in
Determined to be pulled
To uproot you from your life
Giving yourself as a gift of amore

Everything that was once fresh
Soon withers
A natural decay
Before death
Or before being cast away
Like being thrown into a bin
Or thrown onto a compost heap

You move on
Soon aroused and intoxicated
By another free spirit
With her natural fragrance
Or by someone plastic
Virtually manufactured
By the latest fashion
Or perhaps someone fresh
New experiences lived

Will you even remember me?
The original
The free and wildflower
Before being plucked
Placed where you wanted me to be

Like in a bunch of flowers in a vase
Slowly sinking and drowning
Seduced for momentary pleasures
Soon discarded and forgotten

Willow

You are like a weeping widow
Bereft of her lover and soul mate
Tears overflowing and creating a river
Like the pain and sorrow of Niobe
And yet you have many years ahead of you
Instead of standing stooped and worn
Making you old before your time
Like some Victorian crinkled widow
Make yourself radiant and beautiful
Cast away those acidic tears
Branch out and reinvent yourself

Wisteria

You look so glamorous
No one can tell
Just how much support you need
Twisting and turning
Just to manage to get a grip
Should the support you receive stop
I'm afraid you would end up
In a heap on the floor

Witch Hazel

You might look old
Spiny and drooped
Anaemic and withered
But you are wise
Able to invent
Soothing ointments
Essential oils
Which you then use
To relieve the pain of others
Alleviating itchy skin
Even revitalising their appearance
Making them more youthful
Virtually making dreams a reality
And as you unselfishly
Give more and more of yourself away
The more shrivelled looking you become
Almost as though you are willing
To give your life and youth
To make others happy and alive

Yellow Bells

You are bright
All showy and vibrant
Dazzling and colourful
Sexily attracting the birds,
The bees and butterflies
You are anything but shy
As those encounters
Result in the most
Tingling sensations

Yew

Is there any part of *yew*
That is not poisonous?
Virtually every part of *yew*
Is exceptionally toxic

And the only reason
That *yew* are so deadly
Is because everything
Is about *yew, yew, YEW*

Yggdrasil

Imagine a tree so HUGE
That entire worlds exist within it
Branches where mythical creatures live
Including gigantic fire-breathing dragons
Giving rise to the legend of this Ash Tree
Where gods, humans and animals can co-exist
Even sacrificing themselves so that the tree lives on

Imagine a tree so HUGE
That birds build their nests
Raising their young
Protecting them from the giants
Those humans who pollute the air
Making it difficult for trees to prosper
Endangering lives on so many levels

More Books by Mario

Birth Life Burial

This is a poetry book concerning birth, life and death and all the ups and downs our unique adventure brings. There are over 100 poems written in a variety of voices and moods. Poems which are endearing and emotive, some that are humorous and comedic, and others which are thought provoking. Spanning a number of topics including childhood, love, parenthood, betrayal, older age, suicide, and death, these memorable and refreshing poems are varied in form (such as rhyme and free verse) and also in length.

There is also a number of allegory poems. The various poems are presented from different perspectives, such as from the parent or the child, the person proposing, the person being cheated upon, and from an independent/third party point of view. Whatever stage of life you may have reached, you will have experienced some of the emotions or events shared in Birth, Life, Burial.

Buy your copy here: https://amzn.to/31oafSt

Myths and Make-Believe

This is a poetry book concerning myths, legends, fairy tales, and other make-believe characters and fictional entities. There are over 100 poems. Examples of Greek Myth characters includes Zeus and Hera, Atlas, Medusa and the Gorgon sisters, Python, Arachne, the Minotaur and the Labyrinth, the Sphynx, the Kraken, and many more.

There is Audhumbla from Norse mythology. From the Old Testament there are poems about Noah, Lot's wife, Cain from Cain and Able, Lilith, David and Goliath, Salome, Angels, and the Devil. Poems about Legends includes King Arthur, Excalibur, and the Lady of the Lake. There are also poems about Dragons, Fairy Tales, Easter Island, Witches, Black Cats, Monsters, Clowns, Ghosts, Werewolves, and the Tooth Fairy. Finally, there are also poems about places such as Ireland, Prague, Cannock Chase, and castles.

The poems are in a variety of voices, and different moods such as serious, thought-provoking and emotive, or humorous and comedic.

Buy your copy here: https://amzn.to/2VPyLef

Do You Recognise Yourself?

Do You Recognise Yourself? is a colourful, eclectic poetry collection which takes a beautiful, brutally honest and hilarious look at the patchwork of life. Using creative flair and first-rate storytelling skills the author expertly reflects on the weird and wonderful traits of people – both fictitious and real – celebrating the humorous with the irresistible and outing the darker personalities who live and work beside us all.

The author's superb observations of the human psyche, inter-faith relationships, family, writing groups, broken marriages, Brexit, womanisers, anxiety, and even a Wolverhampton Witch are perceptive, thoroughly entertaining and will have you nodding, smiling, empathising and reflecting from beginning to end.

Events, people and situations are embellished, merged and distorted to create a kaleidoscope of rhyme and verse that will resonate with readers from all walks of life. Who knows, you might even recognise yourself in there too.

Buy your copy here: https://amzn.to/3cmAsGM

Animal in YOU?

Mario's fourth published poetry collection, *Animal in YOU?,* is unlike any you have encountered. With his now signature poetry style, Mario sparks ideas, concepts and reflection for the most imaginative of minds.

If you've ever reflected on how deeply the connection between animals and humans run or how many fascinating characteristics we have in common, you'll find much to contemplate in this enigmatic bumper read.

These colourful poems are written in diverse styles (free verse, rhyme, Haiku, allegory and even a sonnet!). Some are humorous, some sad, others hold a direct mirror to ourselves and reflect our best and worst features or those of our friends and foe.

A rich and entertaining collection of over 340 poems you can read and enjoy time and time again.

Buy your copy here: https://amzn.to/2D70f9Q

Glimpses of Epic Greek Myths

Rich in characters and ill-fated storylines, Greek Myth tales have survived for thousands of years. And in this collection, the author draws on ancient dramas and characters to offer a truly fascinating glimpse at pivotal moments in their lives, transformations and deaths. As one would expect in such irresistible Greek tales, there are Gods and Goddesses, a gorgon, cyclopean children, a titan, kings, queens, princes and princesses, a prophetess, sea nymphs, gigantic monsters and warriors. What they get up to and who with will leave a lasting memory and test your moral compass.

Epic tales of some of the lesser-known characters from the world of Greek myth, and those shrouded in mystery, are now brought to life in an irresistibly entertaining and visual manner. Their personalities, motivations, sexual tensions and prowess, their true nature, and their interactions are literally laid bare – in more ways than one. These explosive, moving and tragic legendary sagas will introduce you to a new and intoxicating experience.

However, please open at your peril. It is not for the innocent nor the faint of heart. Full of adult themes and scenes, some explicit in nature, Glimpses of Epic Greek Myths will either make you grateful for your relatively calm and predictable life or force you to unlock and unleash your dark side. The choice is yours.

Buy your copy here: https://amzn.to/3x7lzSV

What Drink Are You?

What does the beverages that you drink
actually reveal about your personality?

Do you drink tea and/or coffee?
Perhaps a vodka or martini?
Are you hip and trendy with a gin?
Or maybe just a beer drinker?

This is a hilarious take
On your characteristics
Just based on what you drink

Over 150 poems.
Including allegory poems.

Find out if you are
Boring and dull
Or sexy, hot and desirable

After reading this collection
Will you stick to your usual drink?
Or will you change your drink?
Hoping for a brand new and invigorating image.

Buy your copy here: https://amzn.to/3i5KdyQ

Political Perspectives

If ever there was a perfect subject for poetry it's politics. Welcome to this satirical, entertaining, humorous, explosive, and highly observational collection of poems to while away the hours. From its origins in Greek Myth and Cleopatra's untimely demise in 30BC to the tumultuous 21st centuries shenanigans, topples from grace, bad decisions, corruption, affairs, scandals and soap operas that continue to occupy our newspapers, gossip columns and TV sets around the globe. Be reminded of the Fat Cats, the Greedy Guts, the Big Wigs, the Unmentionables, and the ludicrous legacies they've left (and would rather forget).

This heady mix of power and politics has something to make everyone smile, fume, and ponder all the cringe-worthy headlines we'd rather forget, including:

- The Prescott punch
- "That woman"
- The Incredible Sulk
- The Dancing Queen
- The Duck House
- That eye test
- And that's before we start on the rest of the world!

Buy your copy here: https://amzn.to/3icNywe

Selections (2021-2022 Edition)

An exciting synopsis of the author's current and future books. With a selection of poems and/or prose from each collection.

Nine published books:
Birth Life Burial
Myths and Make-Believe
Do you recognise yourself?
Animal in YOU?
Glimpses of Epic Greek Myths
What drink are you?
Political Perspectives
Selections (2021/2022 Edition)
What Fruit Are You?

Seven books to be published:
2020: A Year of Heroes
Banned Book of Greek Myth
Banned Book of Poetry
Cyprus Collection
Philosophical Perspectives
Stag Story
What Flower, Bush or Tree Are You?

An inexpensive way to enter a brand new reading experience.

Buy your copy here: https://amzn.to/3kO8JpA

What Cake or Dessert Are YOU?

What does the cake you enjoy eating say about you?

Are you sugary and sweet?
Do you enjoy a sponge cake,
And does that mean you sponge off others?
Do you have spice and bite to your character?
Do you have a crunchy exterior?
But then a soft and melting interior
Do you crumble?
Are you as hard as a meringue?
Or sour and acidic?
Angelic or Devilish?
Are you frosty, or cool and chilled?
Are you a little nutty?
Are you naughty?
Let's get down to the nitty gritty
Are you a bit of a tart?
An inexpensive way to enter a brand new reading
experience.

Buy your copy here: https://amzn.to/3k7EoS1

About the Author

Mario Panayi was born in the UK but visited his relatives in Cyprus every year during his childhood. It was a very different Cyprus in the 1970s and early 1980s compared to now as Cyprus had been invaded in 1974. The visits he made to Cyprus were very influential on Mario, as he witnessed the aftermath of war such as refugees living in tiny accommodation, running water half a day per week which had to be stored for the whole week, no telephones, and of course more than 2,000 people had disappeared, presumed dead. This included two of his cousins.

It made Mario very conscious of how fortunate most people are in life, including himself, and how precious life is. He also forged a close relationship to his relatives in Cyprus. Mario found that being told he couldn't do things just made him more determined to be able to do things. At school, a teacher refused to sign off his university application, explaining that there was no point applying to University because he was not capable academically of getting a degree and would probably not be accepted at University. He applied regardless and got two honours degrees, one postgraduate degree and two Masters degrees, including an MBA.

At a previous job he was told by his manager that he could not write. It was at that point he went on to get his final degree which was a BA (HONS) Philosophy and Creative and Professional Writing, but he never studied poetry.

Mario has found that walking and writing are cathartic and therapeutic.

To date he has published 10 books:

- *Birth, Life, Burial* (2018)
- *Myths and Make-Believe* (2018)
- *Do You Recognise Yourself* (2019)
- *Animal in YOU?* (2020)
- *Glimpses of Epic Greek Myths* (2020)
- *What Drink Are You?* (2020)
- *Political Perspectives* (2021)
- *Selections 2021-2022 Edition* (2021)
- *What Cake or Dessert Are You?* (2021)
- *What Flower, Tree or Bush Are YOU?* (2022)